CW01658680

you are loved

julie ann heath

potters maze limited
leicester

Copyright ©2024 by Julie Ann Heath
ALL RIGHTS RESERVED

No portion of this book may be reproduced, electronically or by any other means, including photocopying, without written permission of the publisher.

First published in United Kingdom in 2024 by
Potters Maze Limited, Leicester LE2 3DA

ISBN: 978-1-7385083-0-3

Printed in U.K.

Love Jonathan x

Once I attended a
gathering of those that,
like me, are trying to
live a life of Love, kindness
and peace, following the
Eternal Light

Many words were spoken
Many fell fallow
Uninspired, I left,

Alone I walked.
What would
God
say to us I wondered
So I asked...

Dear God, Eternal Light,
what would you say to those
that love you and seek your
will?

Over the days ahead
these words of
encouragement
came into
my heart

you are loved

… love never ends

Divine Love is eternal

you are
loved

you are not alone

a circle of
Divine Love
surrounds you

- be still
- breathe
- listen

you are not alone

you are chosen

you are unique

your love matters
your love changes
the world around
you
your love is
beautiful
choose love
everyday

you are
chosen

you are a reflection
of truth

let eternal love work
through you.
like light through a window
you will shine.

you are a reflection of truth

you are a messenger

you have been given
love

accept that love,
share that love
even when it hurts

And love will grow

you are a
messenger of
love

have courage
life brings
challenges

hope is our comfort

perseverance
our friend.

have
courage

have patience

· be still
· breathe

have
patience

do not be afraid

you are not alone

you are loved
love conquers
fear

Do not be
afraid

you have been
tested
And yet you are here
· still listening
· still searching
· still loving

you
have
been
tested

you will be tested...
you know life brings
challenges
always give them much
consideration,
and time in prayer.

Wait for the vision
listen, then rise
gently, with kindness,
energy and hope

you will
be
tested

no one is perfect
but everyone is
precious

remember you are
human
you know you have faults
be aware of them
know them, discover the
truth about you
embrace the whole of you
you are wonderful
be kind to yourself

always be kind

no one is perfect
but everyone is precious
you
are
wonderful
just be
kind
remember
you
are
human
you know
you have
faults
be aware
of them
know them
discover
the truth
about
you
embrace
the
whole
of you

learn how to
say sorry
no. one is perfect

saying sorry is a
strength
forgiveness,
Divine or other,
can heal and
restore
peace

learn how to say sorry

trust in love...

· truth lives eternally
· love lives eternally

We are all connected
by love

trust
in
Love

be confident with your
message of love.
grow strong, be aware of
the world and its ways.
do not be afraid.
try and understand.
look from the other side
look up, look down,
look around.

always
with
Be confident
Be worldly
Strong
GROW
an open
heart

tend to your soul...

you are loved
you are cherished
you are precious
...rest...
listen to your desires
be kind to yourself
be honest
be true
listen to your
needs
share your
dreams with
the Divine Light

tend to your soul

tend to your
relationships
listen carefully
open your heart
try not to judge
~ encourage
just love gently

seasons will come and go
some will flourish
some will be difficult
some will bring loss and pain
Only love brings hope

tend to your relationships

remember humility
is all

you are called by
name not by title or
wealth
All are equal

remember
humility is all

return always to love
dreams and visions
unfold over time, be
patient ~ all can flourish
your influence is love

return always
to love

When we first hear the Divine
voice our heart leaps.

With joy our quest begins,
our faith flourishes
Then,

- So many choices.
- So many roads.
- So many tests.

We search for validation.
We yearn for acceptance.
We wish to be heard.
We long to make a difference.

highs

lows

tears

laughter

delight

darkness

questioning

doubt

peace can evade us

The Divine voice ~

a whisper

Not all things will go
your way.
you cannot fix everything.
you cannot fix everybody.
you can just walk gently
by their side.

When ego is put aside like
light through a window,
even in doubt and
confusion, the Truth
will shine through your
heart and comfort
your soul

Listen the
Divine voice
is calling

1. you shall love the
Lord your God
with all your heart,
and with all your
soul,
and with all your mind,
and with all your
strength

2. you shall love your
neighbour
as yourself

In the garden of
our lives, love,
kindness, and
gentleness are
the trellis of
support. Only with
their presence will we
truly blossom and grow

listen in the darkness
listen in the light
listen with your heart

listen with your soul open your heart see the light in others

you are
loved